W9-AHA-743

16.99

11/11

DEMCO

Spitting Cobra

By Avery Willebrandt

Gareth Stevens
Publishing

Please visit our website, www.garethstevens.com. For a free color catalog of all our high-quality books, call toll free 1-800-542-2595 or fax 1-877-542-2596.

Library of Congress Cataloging-in-Publication Data

Willebrandt, Avery.
Spitting cobra / Avery Willebrandt.
    p. cm. — (Killer snakes)
Includes index.
ISBN 978-1-4339-5651-5 (pbk.)
ISBN 978-1-4339-5652-2 (6-pack)
ISBN 978-1-4339-5649-2 (library binding)
1. Spitting cobras—Juvenile literature. I. Title.
QL666.O64W55 2011
597.96—dc22

2011002876

First Edition

Published in 2012 by
Gareth Stevens Publishing
111 East 14th Street, Suite 349
New York, NY 10003

Copyright © 2012 Gareth Stevens Publishing

Designer: Michael J. Flynn
Editor: Greg Roza

Photo credits: Cover, pp. 1, (pp. 2–4, 6, 8, 10, 12, 14, 16, 18, 20–24 snake skin texture), 5, 6–7, 9, 15 Shutterstock.com; pp. 11, 17 Tom Brakefield/Stockbyte/Getty Images; p. 13 Digital Vision/ Getty Images; p. 19 iStockphoto; p. 21 Dave Hamman/Gallo Images/Getty Images.

Printed in the United States of America

CPSIA compliance information: Batch #CS11GS: For further information contact Gareth Stevens, New York, New York at 1-800-542-2595.

Contents

No Spitting! 4

Spitting Cobras of the World 6

Different and the Same 8

Growing Up 10

Spitting or Spraying? 12

Hit the Target 14

Deadly Bite 16

Spitting Cobras and People 18

The Mozambique Spitting Cobra . . 20

Glossary 22

For More Information 23

Index 24

Boldface words appear in the glossary.

No Spitting!

Spitting cobras are a group of snakes that can shoot **venom** from their **fangs**. They don't do this when they're hunting for food. They only do it to chase away enemies. The venom hurts when it hits an animal in the eyes.

5

Spitting Cobras of the World

Spitting cobras live in hot areas of Africa, Asia, and Australia. They're found in grasslands, plains, and rocky hillsides. The longest type of these snakes is called Ashe's spitting cobra. It can grow to more than 9 feet (2.7 m) long!

Different and the Same

Spitting cobras can be different sizes and colors. Like all cobras, spitting cobras can make the part of their body just below their head wider and flatter. This is called a hood. A cobra's hood makes it look bigger and scarier to its enemies.

Growing Up

Spitting cobras lay eggs in old logs, **termite** nests, and animal **burrows**. Babies are venomous and start hunting right away. While adults hunt mainly at night, young snakes often hunt during the day. Spitting cobras eat small animals, such as lizards, frogs, and mice.

11

Spitting or Spraying?

Spitting cobras don't actually spit their venom. They spray it! The venom is stored in small body parts called glands. The cobras use **muscles** around these glands to push the venom out through holes in their fangs.

Hit the Target

Some spitting cobras can spray their venom up to 10 feet (3 m) away! They're very good at hitting small **targets**. The cobra commonly aims for its enemy's eyes. The venom causes pain and blinds the enemy. This lets the cobra escape.

Deadly Bite

The venom a spitting cobra sprays isn't meant to cause death. However, the snakes do use their venom to kill **prey**. Spitting cobras shoot their venom into prey by biting them. Their fangs are short, but they're sharp enough to break through the animal's skin.

Spitting Cobras and People

People sometimes scare spitting cobras when walking in the wild. It takes just a few seconds for a spitting cobra to spray venom into a person's eyes. The venom can cause blindness if the person doesn't wash it out of their eyes right away.

The Mozambique Spitting Cobra

The Mozambique spitting cobra is one of the deadliest snakes in Africa. It can raise up to two-thirds of its body off the ground. It spreads its hood to look scarier. This snake can hit an animal's eyes from 8 feet (2.4 m) away.

Snake Facts
Mozambique spitting cobra

Length	up to 4 feet (1.2 m)
Color	green-gray, brown, or gray and black
Where It Lives	southern Africa
Eggs	Females can lay up to 22 eggs at one time.
Killer Fact	The Mozambique spitting cobra is easily angered. However, it's known to play dead when facing larger enemies.

Glossary

burrow: an animal home dug into the ground

fang: a long, sharp tooth

muscle: a body part that helps an animal move

prey: an animal hunted by another animal

target: an object to aim at

termite: a small bug that lives in large groups and eats wood

venom: something a snake makes inside its body that can harm other animals

For More Information

Books

Kopp, Megan. *Cobras.* Mankato, MN: Capstone Press, 2011.

Roza, Greg. *Poison! The Spitting Cobra and Other Venomous Animals.* New York, NY: PowerKids Press, 2011.

Websites

The Crocodile Hunter Diaries: Spitting Cobra
animal.discovery.com/videos/the-crocodile-hunter-diaries-spitting-cobra.html
Watch crocodile hunter Steve Irwin get attacked by a spitting cobra.

Fooled by Nature: Spitting Cobra
videos.howstuffworks.com/animal-planet/28417-fooled-by-nature-spitting-cobra-video.htm
Watch a video of a spitting cobra spraying venom at an enemy.

Reptiles: Cobra
www.sandiegozoo.org/animalbytes/t-cobra.html
Learn more about cobras, including spitting cobras.

Index

Africa 6, 20, 21
Ashe's spitting cobra 6
Asia 6
Australia 6
babies 10
blindness 14, 18
colors 8, 21
eggs 10, 21
enemies 4, 8, 14, 21
eyes 4, 14, 18, 20
fangs 4, 12, 16
frogs 10
glands 12
hood 8, 20

hunting 4, 10
lizards 10
mice 10
Mozambique spitting
    cobra 20, 21
muscles 12
pain 14
people 18
prey 16
venom 4, 10, 12, 14,
    16, 18